PROPHET
ADAM

A SERIES ON QURANIC COMPREHENSION -
PROPHETS AND PROPHETHOOD

DR. SYED HAIDER RIZA

Publication: 2022

ISBN Paperback 9780645209181

ISBN Ebook 9780645209174

Published by:

TS Publications

Truth Seekers Foundation

PO Box 498, Craigieburn, VIC 3064, Australia

www.truthseekersfoundation.org

books@truthseekersfoundation.org

CONTENTS

CHAPTER 1: INTRODUCTION & OVERVIEW 1

IMPORTANT POINTS TO LEARN AND PONDER: 2

CHAPTER 2: STUDY OF QURANIC VERSES RELATED TO HAZRAT ADAM 7

A. CREATION OF ADAM AND THE CONCERNED INQUIRY OF ANGELS REGARDING HIS *KHILAFAH* 7

Sura Baqarah (2) 8

B. *SAJDA* OF ANGELS AND THE REBELLIOUS, JEALOUS *IBLEES* 11

Sura Baqarah (2) 12

Sura Hejr (15) 13

Sura A-raf (7) 14

Sura Baqarah (2) 15

Sura A-raf (7) 16

Sura Nisa (4) 18

C. RESIDENCE OF ADAM AND HAWWA IN JANNAH FOLLOWED BY THEIR EXPULSION (FROM THERE) AND IMMEDIATE RETURN (TAWBA) TO ALLAH 19

Sura Baqarah (2) 20

Sura A-raf (7) 20

Sura Taha (20) 21

Sura A-raf (7) 22

Sura A-raf (7) 24

Sura Baqarah (2) 25

D. THE FIRST HUMANS AFTER ADAM AND HAWWA 27

Sura Maedah (5) 27

E. ADVICE OF ALLAH TO THE CHILDREN AND PROGENY OF ADAM 29

Sura Yaseen (36) 29

Sura A-raf (7) 30

CHAPTER 3: SUMMARY AND CONCLUSIONS 33

PREFACE

Dear Readers, we are bringing to you a number of short books (not booklets) compiled as a series on one of the most important Quranic topics of "Prophet-hood and the Lessons from the Lives of Prophets." By the Permission of Allah, these will be followed by similar books based on the Quranic verses related to Akherat and Qiyamah. The initial series on Prophets will cover the life-changing and moral-building lessons acquired from the lives of those Prophets of Allah whose ways and conduct (seerah) are narrated in some detail in our Holy Book. This series will comprise of a collection of seven (7) books, starting from Hazrat Adam, with every book based on the Quranic description of the life of a chosen Prophet. You should find these books significantly different from those already available in the name of life history of Prophets. So, what are the fruits of our efforts, let us describe in some depth.

INTENT

Primary goal and major intent are to keep this series purely Quran-based. Hence, the main feature of this series of books is their complete submission and adherence to the concepts illuminated by the Quranic verses with few but incredibly important and necessary supplements from the *Ahadith* of *Masoomeen* (a.s.). The readers of Quran who deliberate and ponder on the verses know very well that Quran is never interested in telling the history of past nations or lives of noble Prophets in terms of historical events and geographical locations. Quran is completely focussed on the guidance and nurturing of human souls towards the Divine Realities of *Towheed* and

Akherat for which the exemplary features from the lives of Prophets play the important part as role models. Character and conduct of these chosen souls are the major references and manifestations of 'eternal truth.' In the length and breadth of the Holy Book we do not find allusions or discussions about where Hazrat Ibrahim spent the most part of his life, whether the water mass in which Pharaoh (*Firon*) was drowned was river Nile or the Mediterranean Sea or where exactly the nations of *Aad* and *Thamud* were located? These details have been researched and documented by numerous investigators of the holy texts, but Quran is not specific and elaborative in these respects. Our intent is to invariably follow the same approach.

In summary our objectives can be enlisted as:

- Quran is the Book of Life sent for the living soul. It is a crime to remain alienated and aloof from this wonderful gift. Our intent is to remove the obstacles and clarify the ambiguities that apparently force millions of Muslims to stay away from building an active and direct connectivity with Quran.

- Other main intent is to provide our readers with an in-depth and analytical insight about how Quran unfolds the realities of human life while citing the lives of Prophets of Allah as the major reference.

- The third objective is to attract and motivate the thinking and inquisitive minds to enter the realm of Quranic comprehension instead of remaining confined to Quranic reading (*Tilawat*) and *Tajweed*. Quran is for all the humanity and our intent is to emphatically illustrate this fact.

- Another important goal is to educate our readers about the manner of verse-analysis and to develop the ability of extracting the patterns of meanings and relations among the Quranic verses.

APPROACH & SCOPE

The crux of our approach is to accurately follow the Quranic streams while building and fine tuning our discussions. We begin with an introductory chapter which illustrates an overview of the concepts and invigorates many important queries regarding the life of the particular prophet we are going to discuss. As the readers know well that in Quran, the discussion on a Prophet is spread over many Surahs and verses, therefore, in the following chapters or sections our focus will shift upon combining and augmenting those apparently dispersed verses. This task resembles joining the pieces of a puzzle and helps in extracting the complete picture as presented in the Holy Book.

The next major aspect of our approach is focussed on keeping the Quranic message pure i.e., extricating the emerging meanings from the shackles of personal and social influences so that we can adequately connect to the Divine domain of facts. And this is the path that needs to be very carefully traversed, since here lies the tricky terrain where many learned scholars may falter. We have tried our best to not transgress the limits prescribed by the Quranic verses.

In our discussions, we are motivated by the need to retain the interactivity and frankness of discourse. We have tried to cover the maximum possible dimensions of the scope of Quranic verses, and simultaneously concentrated on keeping the discussions well-knitted and conceptually sound. How much this effort is successful, the readers will tell.

As far as the scope of readership is concerned, the intended or expected audience is the aware and inquisitive mind who wants to understand and the honest soul who desires to absorb the Quranic fragrance. Are we sensitive about the age groups? No, really not! Our experience has shown that youth in their grades eleven or twelve are aptly capable of comprehending these ideas. Nevertheless, the discussions are prepared and presented to involve and include the majority who are intellectually capable, sufficiently educated, and mentally alert but still consider themselves alienated from the wonderful and beautiful world of Quran simply because they are not trained as formal religious scholars in seminaries. For this very reason, this book is not written on the pattern of commentaries (Tafaseer) written by religious scholars, rather its scope focusses more on the comprehension and exploration of Quranic concepts instead of thorough lexical analysis and comparison of the viewpoints of Quranic commentators. But it would be a folly to assume that we have neglected the Quranic commentaries of authentic Ulema. As our major reference, we follow the best Quranic researchers like Allamah Mohammad Husain Tabatabaei and Ayatollah Jawadi Amoli.

ASSUMED BACKGROUND OF READERS

The persons who take up this book must not be alien to Quran. It is expected that they have gone through at least once the length of Quran in terms of reading and know about the Surahs and their contents although in a referential manner. It is assumed that the readers have an overview of the major topics discussed in Quran e Kareem which encompass the belief system, deeds, actions and their consequences and the relevant legislations. It is not assumed that the readers are well versed in the Arabic language, or they have read any Quranic *Tafseer* in detail. Simultaneously we are not taking into consideration that our readers are exclusively religious people, but we do expect them to get closer to Quran in terms of reading and pondering once they begin to find the discussions interesting and enriching. Usually in such cases, a profound alteration in the course of life ensues the comprehension.

SUGGESTED SELF-ASSESSMENT

As you progress through these books you will certainly feel a piling up of numerous strains of gnosis (*marefat*). You will begin to feel that your relationship with Quran was quite shallow and superficial till now and gradually the depth and variety of concepts will become overwhelming. Thus, the need will arise for being methodical and organised in your studies. In this regard we shall like to suggest:

- Please maintain a notebook for writing down the learnt concepts in your own words.

- Note down the questions that emerge on the way. These can be sent to the QA section on our website.

- Refer to the verses mentioned and read their Arabic in Quran and try to figure out the meanings word by word. Estimate your capability of finding the meaning without referring to the translation.

- Make a map of the connection of verses in different Surahs and try to figure out the advancement of concepts when different verses are combined.

- Try to make study and learning groups with your friends and family members within which exchange of ideas and mutual discussion becomes possible and enjoyable.

Finally, we shall wish every facility to come your way as you move towards the comprehension and absorption of *Quran e Majeed*. May new ways be opened before the eyes of your heart, and you become eligible for the backing and encouragement of angels who pick you up on their wings/arms and hasten and facilitate your journey towards wisdom (Hikmah) which is the gateway to eternal heaven.

SYED H. RIZA

Rabiul Awwal 1444 (October 2022)

Melbourne, Australia.

CHAPTER 1
INTRODUCTION & OVERVIEW

Before studying the Quranic verses describing various aspects of the events related to Hazrat Adam, we like to present many important concepts that will greatly help in developing a comprehensive Quran based overview regarding the first human on earth. It must be kept in mind that in Quran we do not find any event describing the life of Adam and his wife after descending on earth. All the narrations are connected to their creation and subsequent incidents and issues till their expulsion from the paradise (Jannah). We must be aware that in those few occurrences such fundamentals and core principles are embedded that govern and define human history and destination.

In many places, we pursued our discussion in a question answer format and then returning to the descriptive mode as if trying to follow the mind of an avid reader. We shall be eager to know that how much this approach proved to be successful in enhancing the comprehension. As described in the preface, whole discussion is strictly Quran based and encourages the readers to envision the patterns emerging by combining verses from different surahs of Quran.

IMPORTANT POINTS TO LEARN AND PONDER:

1. Hazrat Adam was the first man in the human race which is currently inhabiting the earth. **Q.** Was he also the first man on earth? **A.** We actually do not know. Why? Because Adam was (born or created) almost 10 thousand years ago, but earth is existing for millions of years.

2. Hazrat Adam was not born of parents, instead he was created from clay (sand + water). Exact nature or mechanism of his creation is not given in the Quranic verses.

3. Did Hazrat Adam came into being alone OR Allah created any companion for him?

A: He was created alone but soon after his creation, he was joined by a female companion, his wife, whose name we know as Bibi Hawwa.

4. Did Hazrat Adam and Hawwa begin their lives from some place on this earth, where we live now?

A: They were allowed to live and reside in the beginning in *Jannah*. This *Jannah* was a place where they could live happily without any toils and pains. As we deduce from the Quranic verses, that Jannah mainly consisted of bodily pleasures and comforts, but did not belong to this earth which we know as our living place. But there was something very peculiar in that *Jannah*. There was a tree about which Allah had not allowed them to have any proximity, it was a "forbidden tree" for Adam and his wife both.

5. Was there any enemy of Adam after his creation or every creature can be considered as his friend and supporter?

A: When Allah ordered all the angels to accept the supreme stature of Adam and do *sajda* before him, there was a *Jinn* among the angels who refused to accept the order of Allah. His name was *Iblees*. Consequently, Allah threw him out of the companionship of angels. He subsequently swore that till the day of Judgement; he will continue to drag the progeny of Adam away from the right path. Due to his wickedness, *Iblees* became *shaytan*. Thus, *shaytan* was the envious opponent of Adam and Hawwa in the beginning and he is the sworn enemy of their children in this worldly life.

6. We heard just now that Iblees was a Jinn! Who are Jinn?

A: *Jinn* are the creatures who are created from the flame of fire. They also exist on this earth, but normally we do not see them. Humans are created from the sand and water. Angels are created from light or some very light stuff that is invisible to our eyes.

7. Did *shaytan* accept Adam and Hawwa being granted the residence in Jannah?

A: No, not at all. He was burning with jealousy against them. Thus, *shaytan* was after them every instant to expel them out of *Jannah* and carry them to a world where he can inflict pain and misery on them.

8. Did he succeed in his mission?

So now we learn an important rule i.e., anyone who disobeys Allah cannot live in *Jannah*; he or she then simply becomes ineligible for such a noble place. Hence, even after death, no man or woman can enter *Jannah* if he/she follows the path of sin.

A: Yes, because he enticed Adam and Hawwa to go near and taste from the forbidden tree. Consequently, Adam and his wife were ordered to go down from Jannah to this material world. In this material world, their children undergo the examination of life. The material life is subjected to all sorts of pains, troubles and finally death besides enjoying many blessings of Allah.

9. How *shaytan* succeeded in making Adam and Hawwa ineligible for Jannah?

A: While in Jannah, Adam and Hawwa were forbidden to go near a certain tree. But shaytan came to them in the disguise of a sincere friend and swore to them that "I am your well-wisher and Allah has only forbidden you from this tree so that you do not become an angel or a creature who can live forever." In this way, they were tricked by *shaytan* to disobey Allah's advice. As soon as they ate from that particular tree, they lost their 'residential status' of *Jannah* and were immediately ordered to go down or descend to the material world. This material world, as we know is the Earth, we live in. *Shaytan* was also banished to the same earth forever with them.

10. What are the consequences of *shaytan's* coming down on earth with Adam and Hawwa?

A: Soon after descending on earth, *shaytan* began to lay his traps and hatch sinister plots against the children of Adam to dissuade them from the path of truth and ways taught by Allah. Many humans got trapped into his devilish net of trickeries and soon his 'family' began to grow. Thus, *shaytan* is not alone, his progeny (from *Jinnat*) and his followers (from men) are also living in this world, and they diligently work to grab the good humans and pull them towards their own sinful and barbaric ways.

11. What is the difference between the *Jannah* in which Adam and Hawwa lived after creation and the *Jannah* which will be granted to a momin after death?

A. Main difference is that the *Jannah* given to a momin will be his reward for faith (*Iman*) and good deeds, but the *Jannah* given to Hazrat Adam was a gift. Hence, a person can leave the Jannah that was gifted to him but the Jannah which is awarded will be his or her own property.

How *shaytan* infiltrates the human soul? Imam Ali (a.s) has given an example of the process of infusion of shaytan and his armies into the human heart and soul. That example is of a bird who builds a nest and rears her chicks on a tree. The bird begins with a single straw. Then slowly adds to it. Once the nest is ready, she lays eggs into it. Then waits until the chicks come out of the eggs. Likewise, shaytan begins by bringing for you a very small sin which you may not consider a serious matter.

[Nahjul Balagha Khutba 4]

12. What was the response of Adam and Hawwa once they were ordered to go down to earth and leave *Jannah*?

A. In contrast to *shaytan*, both Adam and Hawwa immediately sensed and accepted their mistake, repented and were extremely sorry for their negligence. In this respect, humanity is starkly dissimilar to the satanic approach and mindset. The real humans will always accept his or her mistake, repent, ask forgiveness of Allah and correct their ways.

13. Did Allah accept the repentance of Adam and Hawwa?

A: Allah accepted their repentance but did not return them to Jannah. Instead, Allah sent for them the guidance in the form of revelation (*Wahi*) and informed them that this worldly life is their examination and here humanity must strive against the snares of *shaytan* and false temptations of their souls for earning their *Jannah*.

PROPHET ADAM

14.What is the course and syllabus and textbook for the examination of life?

A: All the events in human life consist of their course work and examination questions while Quran is the textbook. Prophets and Imams are the role models and reference for right and wrong. Through the employment of wisdom (*Aql*) and with the help of Divine revelation and the appointed role models, who are *Masoomeen* (a.s) humans can successfully pass the examination of life.

15. What is the role of *shaytan* in our worldly life?

A: He infuses false hopes and mean thoughts into the human soul and thus becomes the main source of our examination. It must be kept in mind that *shaytan* is not given any authority or enforcing power over humans. Therefore, whatever bad deeds we do are our own responsibility.

CHAPTER 2
STUDY OF QURANIC VERSES RELATED TO HAZRAT ADAM

Now, after giving a Quran based introduction to the important derivable and fundamental concepts, we proceed towards a detailed study of the verses in which different events related to the creation of Adam and the beginning of humanity are described. The ensuing discussion is arranged topic-wise for ease of comprehension.

Please keep in mind that along the discussion you will find the explanatory notes interspersed with frequent questions that can come to mind after reading the text of Qur'anic verses followed by their answers.

A. CREATION OF ADAM AND THE CONCERNED INQUIRY OF ANGELS REGARDING HIS *KHILAFAH*

Allah (s.w.t) informed the angels (no consultation) about the creation of Adam (and the humanity to follow him) and appointing him in the earth as (His) Khalifa to which angels raised the question of eligibility. Allah answered them appropriately, angels subsequently bowed down to the choice of Allah and agreed to pay complete respect to the newly created Adam.

Sura Baqarah (2)

V. 30: When said your Rab to the angels, "Indeed I am going to appoint a Khalifa in the earth." They replied (asked), "Will you place someone in the earth who will cause corruption in there and spill the blood, (while) we do your *Tasbih* with praise (*Hamd*) and sanctify you?" He (Allah) replied, "Indeed, I have the best knowledge of what you do not know."

Q 1. Who is a *Khalifa*?

A. *Khalifa* is the representative or who succeeds someone.

Q 2. How angels came to know the negative traits of Adam?

A: There are two possibilities: (a) There were human like creatures before Adam who had behaved in those undesirable and ignominious ways as mentioned by the angels OR (b) Angels were appropriately understanding the deficiencies associated with the creation of Adam which was from dust and water. The material world owing to its serious limitations must be full of conflicts punctuated with lust and cruelty, therefore, any creature surrounded by the materialistic influences should exhibit the inevitable characteristics as mentioned by angels in the verse.

Q 3. Were the angels objecting to their Rab's decision?

A: No! Angels are free from jealousy and ill-feelings. They never take stand against the Order and Will of Allah. As proved in the later verses, they were actually inquiring about what they could not comprehend since to them the status of Khalifa of Allah and the propensities of material body were incompatible. In lieu, the creature who performs *hamd* and *tasbih* seems to be more deserving for this noble rank.

Q 4. What can we infer from the reply of Allah?

A: As can be observed from the reply of Allah that the answer was neither 'yes' nor 'no'. Allah neither rejected the stance of angels nor supported their viewpoint. Instead, the answer was based on something else which pertained to the knowledge of Allah, details to be made evident later.

Now moving on to other verses of Sura Baqarah.

V. 31: And He (Allah) taught Adam all the Asma then presented them to the angels and asked them, "inform me of these Asma if you are truthful (in your statement)."

Explanation:

a) Here Allah mentioned 'Adam' as the name of the first human who was chosen by Him to become his Khalifa in the earth (and Universe).

b) In this verse we must note the difference in receiving of the Asma between Hazrat Adam and the angels. When mentioned for Adam, the Quranic word is " علّم "which means 'He taught thoroughly' while when the same *Asma* were referred for angels, the Quran says "عرضهم" that is, 'presented to them or placed upon them'. This change in the manner of receipt tells a whole lot about the difference in the calibre of Adam and the angels with respect to acquiring knowledge and gaining authority over the realities of life OR the secrets of nature.

Here again a couple of questions are coming to mind. Let's try to find their answers.

Q 5. What are *Asma*?

A. *Asma* literally means "Names". But simply telling the names of few important things in the form of words does not make a man *Alim* or knowledgeable. Therefore, here *Asma* refers to the realities of persons, things and objects existing in the Universe and system of life. And since Adam was taught about all the *Asma*, hence it means that the doors of true knowledge of everything were opened for Adam and humanity at the time of their creation.

Q 6. Why Allah interconnected the demand for information about *Asma* from the angels to their truthfulness?

A. Since the angels inquired about the eligibility of Adam regarding his elevation to the lofty status of *Khalifa* of Allah, therefore, Allah explained to them the merit of Adam by putting up this test of the knowledge of *Asma*. In this way, Allah made them aware of the conclusive and immensely important fact that the station of Khalifa requires ILM (true knowledge and wisdom) as the main qualification while worshipping with *Hamd* and *Tasbih*, despite their nobility are not the sufficient qualities.

Returning to the Quranic verses.

V. 32: They replied, "You are Exalted, there is no knowledge for us except what you have given to us. Indeed, you are all Knowing and Wise."

V. 33: (Then Allah) said, "O Adam! Inform them (angels) about their Asma." Thus, when he informed them of their Asma then Allah said (concluded), "Have I not told you that I know the best about hidden realities of the heavens and the earth, and I know everything that you manifest or keep hidden."

Explanation:

a) Now it becomes evident to the angels that the superiority is for ILM (of Asma), and after realising this fact, they accepted their incapability to rise up to the required standard.

b) Allah provided a complete and satisfying proof to the angels of the capabilities of Adam when He asked Adam to inform the angels about "their" or angels' *Asma*. This is very enlightening since in fact, Adam informed the angels about their own reality! This was the proof enough which left no option for the angels but to bow down before the greatness of Adam.

B. *SAJDA* OF ANGELS AND THE REBELLIOUS, JEALOUS *IBLEES*

Angels were ordered to do a *sajda* as the mark of ultimate respect and loyalty to 'the Adam' who has the knowledge of *Asma*. But there was an *Iblees* hidden among the ranks of angels yearning for his own goals. His ambitions were decimated when Adam was elevated to the status of *Khalifa* (of Allah). Consequently, the superiority complex and the fire of jealousy engulfed the soul of *Iblees*, and he signed upon his own 'destruction' by standing against the Order of Allah and refusing to bow in *sajda* before Adam. It is highly noticeable that *Iblees* despite transforming into *shaytan* never doubted the *Towheed* (Monotheism) and he was also a believer in the resurrection (*Qiyamah*). His destruction was not caused by the faulty belief system but diseases in the soul. In other words, lack of morality (*Akhlaq*) was the major cause of his downfall. A pertinent lesson for us to be extremely heedful about *Tazkeya* of our *Nufus*.

This section will be covered with the help of many surahs of Quran e kareem. The respected readers are requested to carefully follow the method of connecting the verses from different places and the emerging of thought patterns.

Sura Baqarah (2)

V. 34: And when We ordered the angels to do *sajda* before Adam, they all prostrated (performed *sajda*) except *Iblees*. He refused and exhibited arrogance (Istekbar ; استکبار) and he 'was' among the *kafereen*.

Explanation:

a) Kafir is the one who hides or denies. Hence kafereen are those men and women who refuse to accept the message of Allah sent through His prophets and found in His books. This term also applies to the group of people who deny the signs (Aya~t) of Allah present everywhere in the world of creation and furnish clear proofs of the presence, authority, and magnificence of Almighty, the Everlasting.

b) When the angels were provided with the appropriate answer to their query, they were ordered by Allah the Almighty to do a *sajda* before Adam. Obviously this *sajda* was not that of worship, but for expressing an immense respect for Adam by the order of Allah. But at this instant, a strange situation arose when one personality among the angels refused to accept the order of Allah! The name of that person was *Iblees*, and he was a *Jinn* residing for many thousand years among the angels and was counted one among them. The mentioning of the fact that Iblees was a *Jinn* and not an angel can be found in the verse 50 of Sura Kahaf (18).

c) When *Iblees* tried to stand against the command of Allah, it was declared that 'he **was** among the 'kafereen' and not that 'then he became a kafir.' This peculiar way of identifying the personality of

Iblees tells us that *Iblees* was only apparently an obedient servant of Allah while in his heart, he was a *kafir*! How can it be? Because during all those thousands of years he was harbouring the desire to attain some high rank in the kingdom of angels, but when Allah announced His *Khilafat* for Adam, all his expectations were smashed, and his innate vindictive qualities punctuated by self-praise, vain pride and jealousy erupted into prominence.

d) '*Istekbar*' is a term that must be clearly understood. It means that a person wants to show himself big OR he wants to acquire a higher and lofty status to which he does not belong. **[Explanation ends]**

The event related to *Iblees* and his transformation into *shaytan* are discussed in appreciable detail in the verses of Quran and considered as one of the most important topics related to human origin. Why *shaytan* is important to humans? Because he is our declared enemy. Here we are including the verses from Sura Hejr to illustrate the deep animosity of *shaytan* towards the descendants and future generations of Adam till the day of *Qiyamah*!

Sura Hejr (15)

V.30: So, all the angels did *sajda* (prostrated) (before Adam).

V.31: Except Iblees; he refused to do *sajda* with the others.

V.32: He (Allah) asked, "O Iblees, what is the matter with you that you are not with the

sajedeen." [*sajedeen* is plural and refers to all those who obeyed Allah's orders and did *sajda* before Adam?]

V.33: (Iblees) replied, "It is not for me (not worthy of me) to do sajda for a *bashar* (human) whom You have created from the dry, swishing clay moulded from the black mud." [*Bashar* refers to the apparent or outwardly features and existence of humans. Mainly refers to the material self.]

The arrogance (*istekbar* : استکبار) of Iblees exhibited in his refusal to bow down to Adam is described in many Surahs. For example, in the verse 12 of Sura A~raf we find a clearer reason for his disobedience when he cited the materials used in the physical creation of Adam and himself as the criterion of superiority.

Sura A~raf (7)

V. 12: (Allah) said, "Who or what has stopped you from prostrating when I have commanded you (to do so)?" He (Iblees) replied, "I am superior to him since you have created me from fire and him from clay."

Here arises a very important question. Let's search for its answer.

Q 7. Iblees declared fire as superior to clay but is that true and a stance based on facts?

A. Iblees committed grave errors on two accounts i.e., spiritually, and physically both. His main mistake was that he considered Adam as 'only' clay and nothing more or just a being confined within material bondages. He completely ignored the spiritual supremacy of Adam that was demonstrated through his capability to acquire " ILM of *Asma*". Secondly, he did not realize that even from the material perspective, clay is better than fire on many accounts like, (i) Lots of things can grow and prosper in clay, but they will be burnt and perished in the fire, (ii) clay when thrown upon a burning fire, can extinguish it but not vice versa. So, in many ways, clay is superior and more beneficial than fire. Hence, the conclusion of Iblees was fundamentally wrong.

When Iblees exhibited his recalcitrance against the order of Allah, he was thrown out of the companionship of angels. But did he feel any shame? Not at all, instead his rebellion grew into jealousy without bounds. From the verses of Sura Baqarah, we can learn about the events soon after the refusal of Iblees to do *sajda* before Adam.

Sura Baqarah (2)

V.34: (Allah) said (in immediate response to Iblees's denial), "Get out from it (companionship of angels), for you are certainly cursed and rejected."

V.35: And surely, upon you is the curse ('Lanat') till the day of judgement."

V.36: [Iblees did not exhibit any remorse, instead demanded shamelessly,] "O my Rab! Then reprieve me till the day of their resurrection."

V.37: He (Allah) replied, "You are from the reprieved ones."

V.38: "till the day of an appointed time."

Explanation:

a) *Lanat* (لعنت) is in fact the deprivation of mercy of Allah. *Lanat* does not mean that the affected person will be deprived of food and oxygen, instead, the main consequences of *Lanat* are being divested of *Hidayat* and the *Toufeeq* to perform good deeds.

b) It is really amazing that *Iblees* did not feel any shame in blatantly refusing to obey the command of Allah! After this act, Iblees transformed into shaytan. But why? If we ponder a bit deeply then there is an answer which also constitutes a very important lesson for us i.e., if a person is overwhelmed by his self-aggrandizement, boastful propensities and burns in the fire of jealousy then he can commit the most heinous deeds like confronting his Creator as witnessed in this case of Iblees.

c) Iblees requested Allah for sparing him from the ultimate punishment till the day of judgement i.e., when *Qiyamah* will happen, and all the humanity will be called for accountability. But for what? To prey upon the generations of Adam and entice them to go astray from the ways of Allah and persuade them on the path to hell.

d) Allah accepted the request of Iblees for a *reprieve* but not did not accept his demand completely. *Iblees* demanded the allowance time till the day of resurrection, but Allah spared him till 'an appointed time.' What is that appointed time? Allah has the best knowledge but surely it is before Qiyamah. **[End of explanation]**

We have talked about the deep-rooted animosity and hatred of Iblees for Adam and his progeny, but one connected aspect remains to be addressed, that is, what are the diabolical plans *shaytan* has in store for the humans? Our Holy Book informs us in very clear terms of the anti-human schemes spoken out loudly by *Iblees* right at the dawn of humanity. We are fortunate to know the strategy of our sworn enemy before entering the battlefield of life. Therefore, these plans must be thoroughly comprehended, and it is obligatory upon us to remain on guard for adequate protection against falling into the devilish traps. We shall present those plans of Iblees from two places in Quran e Kareem.

Sura A-raf (7)

Verses 16, 17: [Now Iblees manifested his evil plans] and claimed, "(O Allah) as you have led me astray, I shall certainly sit for them (humanity) on

Sirat e Mustaqeem. Then I shall surely come to them from their front and from their back and from their right side and from their left side and You will not find the majority of them thankful (shakereen, شاكرين).”

Explanation:

a) It must be clear that *Iblees* and his cohorts cannot sit on *Sirat e Mustaqeem* because it is the highway towards Allah populated by those *Bandegan* who are purified and chosen by Allah Himself. In the Quranic terminology such pure ones are known as *Mukhlaseen* (مخلصين) and upon whom *Iblees* has no influence whatsoever. Therefore, *Iblees* exists everywhere before and up to *Sirat e Mustaqeem* but not on it.

b) *Iblees* has mentioned four sides or dimensions of attack on the children of Adam. Very interestingly, upside and downward directions are left open by him. In addition, he exhibited his main intent as keeping away the humans from *shukr* or being thankful to Allah. Hence, humans can counter *Iblees* by raising up their hands in *Dua* and prayers and bowing down to Allah in *sajda*. *Sajda* is an act which greatly minimises the effects of satanic whisperings. In short, humans have three main weapons to counter the trickery of *shaytan*: (1) *Dua* when we lift our faces and hands upwards to beseech Allah for His mercy and forgiveness (2) *Sajda*, when we put down our faces and important organs on earth to express our utmost humility and sanctify him while turning downwards. (3) *Shukr*, always remembering the blessings of Allah, utilising them according to His Will and Preferences and remaining thankful to Him. **[End of explanation]**

Sura Nisa (4)

V. 118: (Rebellious and cursed *shaytan*) who said (declared his policy of war against the humanity), "(O Allah) I shall definitely grab a certain number of Your *Ibad*."

V.119: (Shaytan continued), "And I shall surely lead them astray and lure them (into false hopes and carnal desires) and (once they are in my fold) they will slit the ears of the cattle and I shall order them to alter the creation of Allah." And whoever accepts and adopts *shaytan* as his *wali* (guardian) instead of Allah, then definitely he has suffered an open and huge loss.

V.120: (And *shaytan* only) presents to them (false) promises and deludes them, and the promises of *shaytan* are nothing but complete deception.

Explanation:

a) Ibad' is the plural of 'Abd (عبد)' which means the person whom Allah has created as a human and blessed him or her with numerous bounties. An '*Abd*' is expected to return the loving gestures and offerings of his Creator through obedience and sincere servitude. Please note that in our opinion, translating 'Abd' as a servant or slave is conceptually wrong and contradicts the spirit of creation of humanity.

b) In many places in Quran like the mentioned verses of Sura Nisa, we find the cards of *shaytan* to be played against humanity as openly manifested. That's why *shaytan* is our 'open enemy' and it is quite a shame for the children of Adam to fall in his traps even after knowing his weapons and intentions.

c) The main thought striking our minds, after reading these verses, is that on what grounds *shaytan* is making such tall claims of grabbing his portions from the humanity and dragging men and women through the filth of morbid character and detestable deeds? It can be inferred from many verses of Quran and the words of Imam Ali (a.s) in *Khutba Qasea* (Nahjul Balaghah) that the claim of *shaytan* was basically a hoax! *Shaytan* was never given any authority over Adam and his children! He can only throw evil thoughts or whisperings (waswasa, وسوسه) towards humans and it is up to humans to accept or reject the invitations of *shaytan*. Additional available facility to humans is that of *Tawba* (repentance) and *Maghferat* (forgiveness) if they sincerely return to Allah after sinning. But unfortunately, despite being in an advantageous position, scores of humans have been blinded by the trickeries of *shaytan* resulting in their lives robbed of Divine guidance and mercy and their souls eventually dragged towards hell fire!

d) Our Imams have also expressed their frustration about the humans who keep on falling into the traps of *shaytan* despite numerous opportunities set in place by the Creator to nullify satanic venom. Like Imam Sajjad (a.s) saying that I am astonished by the person whose one overwhelms his ten. When inquired about the seemingly puzzling sentence, Imam explained that Allah offered minimum of ten rewards for one good deed while the maximum punishment for a sin is one to one only. So how a person still ends up with his sins more than his good deeds? [**End of explanation**]

C. RESIDENCE OF ADAM AND HAWWA IN JANNAH FOLLOWED BY THEIR EXPULSION (FROM THERE) AND IMMEDIATE RETURN (TAWBA) TO ALLAH

Once the issue of creation of Adam and his appointment as the Khalifa was settled for the angels, Adam was given the 'residential place' in Jannah. But at this beginning juncture of his life, he was not alone. He was joined by a female companion. Her exact creation and name are not mentioned in the Quranic verses, but we know these things from the *Riwayat* of AhlulBait (a.s). Thus, began the humanity through the father (Adam) and the mother (Hawwa). Noticeably, the beginning did not begin from the earth but from *Jannah* and that too, under a strict condition. Let's learn about these illuminating events from the verses of *Quran e Majeed.*

Sura Baqarah (2)

V. 35: And We said, "O Adam, you and your wife (Hawwa) may reside in the *Jannah* and eat from wherever you like, in abundance. And do not go near this tree then you both will be among the *zalimeen* (unjust)."

Q.8: Who are in fact unjust or *Zalimeen?*

A: *Zalimeen* are those people who function in an unjust way or due to sins they throw their own souls in the throes of darkness (*Zulumat* : ظلمات). Another instance of *zalimeen* are those people who obstruct the progress and corrupt the lives of other humans. Allah has described shirk (شرک) or polytheism as the worst form of *zulm* in Sura Luqman, verse 13.

Sura A~raf (7)

V. 19: And O Adam you reside with your wife in the Jannah and eat from wherever you both like but do not go near this tree since then you both will become from *zalimeen.*

Sura Taha (20)

V.117: And We said, "O Adam, surely this (*shaytan*) is an enemy of you and your wife, thus, (beware) lest he removes you both from the *Jannah* and then you would suffer (hardship)."

V.118: "Indeed, here (in *Jannah*) you will not be affected by hunger nor face the problem of nakedness."

V.119: "And certainly you would not suffer (here) from the 'thirst' or the sun's heat."

Explanation:

a) By combining all these verses, we can understand that Adam and his wife were treated with honour and given a noble place to live which is called *Jannah* or paradise. But the noticeable fact is that the facilities in that paradise were similar to the perfect material comforts a subset of which can be found on this earth. There is no mention of spiritual or intellectual activity and growth of the newly created humans! And that was actually the domain where Adam became restless and exactly there the *shaytan* struck.

b) When the permission to live in *Jannah* was granted, it was accompanied by a warning and an advice that could not be ignored. The warning was related to *shaytan* who had already revealed his hatred and intriguing schemes for Adam and his future generations. Allah's advice to them was to remain at a safe distance from a certain tree in the *Jannah*. Hence the fate and future of Adam in *Jannah* was hanging in a delicate balance. If *shaytan* could succeed in bringing Adam and his wife near the forbidden tree and entice them into tasting it, then the time of Adam in *Jannah* would be over, and he will be forced to descend into a world of toils and hardships. [**End of explanation**]

We all know what happened next, and that Adam and his wife were tricked by *shaytan* to act against the advice of Allah as a consequence of which they immediately lost their residence in *Jannah* and ordered to go down to earth and experience a life fraught by a myriad of problems and sufferings. Now we shall study the Quranic verses from Sura A~raf which describe the tricks of *shaytan* for alluring Adam and Hawwa towards the forbidden tree followed by the Divine order for them to leave Jannah and descend to earth for a temporary residence.

Sura A~raf (7)

V. 20: And then *shaytan* made for them an (evil) suggestion [whispered to them] with the intention of exposing for them their hidden shame. He said, "Your Rab has not forbidden you both from going near this tree but for the reason (apprehension) that you two may become angels or you both may live forever."

V. 21: And swore to them both that surely, I am a sincere guide and advisor for you.

V. 22: Thus, he caused them to go astray by deception (or deceit) and they both tasted from the tree and (immediately) their shame was manifested to them, and they began to cover themselves by the leaves (of trees) in Jannah. And their Rab called out to them, "Have I not forbidden you about going near that tree and warned you both that certainly *shaytan* is an open enemy for you?"

Explanation:

a) The scheme of *shaytan* comprised of a two-pronged attack. As the first strike, he ornamented the temptations of becoming angels and attaining the eternal life for the newly created humans. Both these prospects were dear to Adam and hence they were forced to listen to the whispering of *shaytan*. To reinforce his venomous argument, *shaytan* swore to them both about his sincerity. Since Adam and Hawwa had not witnessed anyone deceiving in this manner, they fell into this trap and went near the forbidden tree.

b) The main aim of *shaytan* was to expose the personal shame or nakedness to Adam and Hawwa. This has been an extremely poignant issue in the history of humanity and reminds us of the most vulnerable aspect of human physical nature; more on it later.

Q.9: Should not Adam and Hawwa abstain from the satanic recommendations since they were already warned by Allah about him?

A: This stage of *shaytan* alluring the first humans is especially instructive because it illuminates the main weakness of humans which is easily exploitable. That weakness is the earnest desire of humans to obtain a perfect and eternal life without any shortcomings and deficiencies. Hence, they think angels as better than them when they compare their material bodies to their composition from something delicate and non-destructible. But the setback experienced by Adam and Hawwa teaches us that humans must strictly adhere to the instructions and guidance of Allah while ignoring all the temptations brewing up in their souls for eternal happiness since these are the propensities which can be exploited by *shaytan* to indulge them in falling in his traps and following the destructive ways.

Q 10: Adam was given the ILM of Asma earlier. Why did that ILM not stop him from accepting the deceptive arguments of *shaytan*?

A: There are many levels of answering this important question, but we shall choose the easier answer. Success of *shaytan* in deceiving Adam and Hawwa despite Adam having ILM of *Asma*, proves to us that mere ILM or knowledge is not the guarantor of protection from satanic snares. It is in fact, *Tazkeya* and *Iman* which ensure the presence of adequate defence lines against infusions and incursions of *shaytan*.

As soon as Adam and Hawwa realised their mistake and observed the sudden change in their state of living, they felt sincerely ashamed and returned to Allah asking for His mercy and forgiveness (*Rehmat* and *Maghferat* : رحمت و مغفرت) without displaying any hint of anger towards Allah. This quality of returning towards Allah once a person finds himself astray is called "*Towba*." *Towba* (توبہ) or repentance is the main quality that distinguishes true humans from the followers of *shaytan*. The 'army' of *shaytan* following the footsteps of their leader never feel any compunction after committing wrong and shameful deeds while the children of Adam always return to Allah seeking His *maghferat* whenever they commit any wrongdoing. In Sura A-raf we are also told about a very precious Dua recited by Adam and Hawwa which became the reason for acceptance of their *Towba*.

Sura A-raf (7)

V. 23: They both implored, "O our Rab, we have wronged ourselves and if you do not grant us your *maghferat* and mercy, then surely we shall be among the losers."

V. 24: (Allah) said, "Go down (to the Earth), you all; some of you will be the enemy of others and for you there is a residing and provision in the earth for a stipulated time."

V. 25: Allah continued, "In it (Earth) you will live and in it you will die and from it you will be brought forth (On the day of Judgement or *Qiyamah*)."

Explanation:

In the Dua recited by Adam and Hawwa mentioned in verse 23 they are stating the fact that if a person knowingly or mistakenly ignores the advice or order of Allah, he deviates from the path of safety and salvation. At that very instant, he or she must return to Allah and request earnestly for His *Rehmat* and *Maghferat* without which all the creatures are losers and destitute. Devoid of *Rehmat* and *Maghferat* their material fortune becomes totally immaterial and irrelevant for their ultimate salvation. **[Explanation ends]**

Allah never rejects those who intend to come back on the right path and make efforts to amend and improve. Hence, the sincere prayers of Adam and Hawwa bore fruit and Allah accepted their *Towba* as mentioned in Sura Baqarah.

Sura Baqarah (2)

V. 37: Then Adam received from his Rab (some) words and (then) He accepted his repentance. Indeed, He is the Acceptor of repentance and Raheem.

Q 11: If Allah accepted the *Towba* of Adam and Hawwa, then why He did not reinstate their position in *Jannah*?

A: As mentioned in verse 30 of Sura Baqarah that Adam was made a *Khalifa* for the earth which means that according to the Divine plan his real destination was earth. But his brief stay in *Jannah* and deception of *shaytan* taught him very important lessons for his coming life in the material world. Another important fact is that Allah wants Adam and his children to earn *Jannah* through their noble faith and righteous deeds. That *Jannah* will be theirs forever.

Q 12: Due to descendance of Adam and Hawwa, we as their children also find ourselves on earth. Is our living time on earth long, short, or very long?

A. In comparison to the real life (in *Akherat*), life in Dunya is very short. Thus, against any problem encountered in worldly life we should remind ourselves that this is a passing phase of very short duration and will terminate soon. As a believer (*momin*) we must have a strong faith that for *momineen* Allah has saved lots and lots of blessings in Akherat.

Q 13: Allah has mentioned that humans will be mainly enemies or adversaries of each other during their earthly life. In contrast, can there be any true friends or sincere friendship among humans during their lives on earth?

A. The enmity and hostility of humans against each other is an obvious and undeniable fact of human life, as witnessed on this earth. But there are true and loyal friendships as well. The main and binding condition for blessed relationships is that believers connect together while seeking the pleasure of Allah and according to the sunnah of *Masoomeen* (a.s). Thus, only that friendship or relation is true and surviving which is established for the love of Allah.

D. THE FIRST HUMANS AFTER ADAM AND HAWWA

Adam and Hawwa began their lives on earth with their *Towba* accepted which enabled them to receive Divine guidance or *Hidayat* from Allah in the form of inviolable rules and principles. The next main question that comes in the mind is about the first children of Adam and Hawwa i.e., how the humanity grew and expanded on this earth. How many children were born to them? Actually, we do not know, but Quran has told us about *Habeel* and *Qabeel*; probably the first born children of Adam and Hawwa. There are many lessons that can be drawn from the small narration of *Habeel* and *Qabeel* as told in Sura Maedah (5) which we now intend to discuss. The description begins from verse 27.

Sura Maedah (5)

V. 27: And recite to them the news of the two sons of Adam with truth when they both offered a sacrifice (before Allah), but it was accepted from one of them and not accepted from the other. He (whose sacrifice was rejected) declared that I shall kill you. The other (Habeel) replied, "Allah only accepts from the *muttaqeen*." [*Muttaqi* = God conscious. The main quality of a God-conscious person is that he or she will never indulge or involve in any *haram*, or a forbidden act as prohibited by the Divine laws.]

V. 28: (*Habeel* continued), "If you extend your hands towards me for killing, I am not going to raise my hands with the intention to kill you. Indeed, I fear Allah, Rab of all the worlds."

V. 29: (*Habeel* further said), "And surely, I want that you accumulate my sins with yours and become one of the companions of the fire (Hell). And that is the just reward for *zalimeen*."

V. 30: (But still) the Nafs of (Qabeel) prompted him to murder his brother whom he eventually killed and ended up among the losers (خاسرین).

V. 31: [After killing Habeel, Qabeel was at a loss about what to do with his dead body?] Thus, Allah sent a crow searching in the ground to show him how to hide the corpse of his brother. Then he cried, "Woe on to me! Have I been more miserable than this crow that I (learn from him) to hide the body of my brother?" And then he ended up being regretful and ashamed.

Explanation:

a) Humanity begins with enmity among real brothers resulting in the murder of the nobler soul. The main difference mentioned between the successful and the loser is *Taqwa*. *Taqwa* means consciousness of Allah which implies that a momin must always visualizes himself in front of the observation of Allah. Thus, *taqwa* is a quality. *Taqwa* is the mandatory requirement for the acceptance of our deeds in the presence of Allah as told to us in the verse 27.

b) Lower than a crow! The verse 31 informs us that *Qabeel* was totally in dark about disposing off the corpse of his slain brother. It was the first dead body in the human history and no previous example was there before *Qabeel* regarding the burial practices. But he was not taught about this tradition through an angel instead a crow became his teacher. This is a very striking observation which tells us that every person gets his teachers according to his level.

c) These verses also educate us about the fundamental principle that *zalim* is the ultimate and eternal loser irrespective of what happens to the sufferer or *mazloom*. Verse 29 quotes *Habeel* as saying that if *Qabeel* kills him then he (Qabeel) will not only carry his own sins but will be burdened by all the sins and faults of *mazloom* (Habeel).

This indeed is a grave situation and highly undesirable ending for anyone inclining towards committing an unjust act or *zulm* on any human being.

E. ADVICE OF ALLAH TO THE CHILDREN AND PROGENY OF ADAM

Alongside the events of Adam, Quran also mentioned the address of Allah to the children of Adam or Bani-Adam. There are many verses which speak about Allah directly giving advice to the humanity like the two verses of Sura Yaseen (36).

Sura Yaseen (36)

V.60: Have I not taken oath from you, O Bani-Adam that you will not worship (and obey) *shaytan*, surely, he is your open (and declared) enemy.

V.61: And instead, worship Me. This is *Sirat e Mustaqeem.*

Explanation:

a) These verses emphasize the need for humanity to take proper guard against *shaytan* who never abstains from his hideous efforts aimed at discouraging and ultimately diverting the humanity from the right path or *sirat e mustaqeem.*

b) These brief verses of Sura Yaseen also define for us the true definition of worship or *bandagi.* We cannot and should not consider ourselves as the *Abd* of Allah irrespective of practical demonstration of our belief and faith in the examination of life. As described by Imam Mohammed Baqir (a.s) that you are the *Abd* of whom you give place in your heart and follow in deeds and actions.

Thus, humans can worship *shaytan* if they honour his values and follow his infusions. **[Explanation ends]**

In Sura Al-A-raf starting from verse 26 and onwards, Allah addresses the children of Adam or humanity at large, directly and gave them some very important pieces of advice and guidance. This is surely an honour for us, the humans.

Sura A-raf (7)

V. 26: O children of Adam, indeed we have sent down for you the clothing which conceals your shame and is an adornment for you; (but) the clothing of *taqwa* that is better. Those are from the signs of Allah so that you may be heedful.

V. 27: O children of Adam, let not *shaytan* tempt you as he removed your parents (Adam and Hawwa) from *Jannah* (when) he caused them to lose their dressing so that their private parts may become visible. Indeed, he and his armies watch you from the places (and dimensions) you do not perceive. Indeed, we make all the tribe of *shaytan* the guardian of disbelievers.

Q 14. Can a Muslim be disbeliever?

A. First we have to find the definition of a disbeliever. Disbelievers are those people who do not accept the orders of Allah. There are many Muslims who do not believe in the dictates and orders of Allah in their hearts which becomes manifest when they are involved in open sinning. These Muslims are counted among disbelievers.

Continuing with the verses of Sura A-raf.

V. 28: When they commit immorality (and obscenity) they say, "We have found our forefathers doing these acts and Allah has ordered it." Say (O prophet), "Allah never orders for immoral and obscene things. Do you say about Allah what you do not know?"

Q 15: We also inherit many customs and traditions from our forefathers. Should we accept these blindly (without scrutiny or thinking) or selectively or based on some criteria?

A: Our fathers are not infallible, and hence there are chances of errors and mistakes. Therefore, whatever we have inherited from them in the name of customs and traditions, be it religious or cultural, should be carefully studied. The acceptance must be based on sound criteria which should be derived from our Islamic and Quranic teachings. If these customs collide with the teachings of Quran, then we must leave and reject these immediately.

V. 31: O children of Adam, take your adornments at the time of every masjid and eat and drink but do not be a spendthrift. Indeed, Allah does not like those who spend excessively (waste the resources).

V. 32: (O Prophet) say, "Who has forbidden the *zeenat* of Allah which He has brought forth for His *Bandegan* and the pure and lawful (Halal) things from the sustenance (*rizq*) ?" Tell (them), "These (blessings) are for the *momineen* in Dunya and exclusively for them in Akherat."

V. 33: Say, "Indeed my Rab has declared *haram* (a) all the immoralities (*fawahish*) whether it is manifest or hidden, and (b) sinning and (c) oppression without justification; and (d) that you commit any shirk with Allah about which He has not sent any clear evidence and (e) that you say about Allah which you do not know."

Explanation:

a) Zeenat means adornments: it includes extra items or things used in addition to normal dress for decoration or beautifying. We must note that Allah has recommended us to do *zeenat* at the time of salat like wearing neat clothes (not fancy garments) and use perfumes and fragrance. Otherwise, *zeenat* is mostly a show-off and an effort to grab other's attention which is essentially a sin.

b) Masjid: The place where you perform sajda (or where you offer salat).

c) Riya-kari (ریا کاری) is Ostentation: the showy display of wealth or any asset with the intention to impress others and grab their attention for self-praise.

d) Fawahish (فواحش) means immoral and obscene acts and thoughts. It covers all the acts and behaviours which should not be openly displayed and exhibited or talked about.

CHAPTER 3
SUMMARY AND CONCLUSIONS

So, after going through the verses spread out in the five different Surahs of Quran e Majeed we have been able to derive many fundamental rules and important principles governing the human life on earth and the potential of humanity as the Khalifa of Allah. We have observed that Quran has laid great emphasis on the beginnings of humanity and made clear for us the major stakeholders in this complex system of life who are: humans, angels and *shaytan*.

Angels are our supporters and helpers if we stick to the path of acquiring ILM of Asma while *shaytan* is our companion if we ignore the advice of Allah given to us through His Prophets and go near the forbidden tree of material pleasures and worldly desires. We must beware that ILM of Asma is not like studying in an institution be it university or seminary that mainly involves reading, writing, teaching, and discussion. ILM of Asma is absorbing the ultimate realities of life by the human soul and demands intensive nurturing and developing of the *Nafs* for receiving the Divine messages and inspirations.

Especially worth remembering are the verses we discussed in the final section in which Allah directly addresses the children of Adam (Bani Adam) and gives them advice about following the path of chastity and abstain from pursuing the lustful pleasures since these pursuits will enable *shaytan* to deprive them of their dressing both in physical and spiritual terms. Physical exposure of personal private parts and the body takes away the important quality of mindfulness and remembrance of Allah (zikr) while spiritually the seed of *Taqwa* can never take root in such a soul. So human beings, by this we mean every human and not only Muslims, must always remember and honour the words of their *Rab* and faithfully practice the most important advice for their lives.

We earnestly hope that this effort, not voluminous but still worthy in meaning and depth, will find favourable response from our esteemed readers and we shall be eagerly waiting for your questions and comments.

Allah bless you with the best bounties of *Dunya* and *Akherat*.